Yellow Pussy Flower

a gift it's how he acts

Anastacia Burrell

 pencil

ISBN 978-93-5667-058-7

Published in India 2022 by Pencil

Contributors:
Co-Author: Anastacia Burrell

A brand of
One Point Six Technologies Pvt. Ltd.
123, Building J2, Shram Seva Premises,
Wadala Truck Terminal, Wadala (E)
Mumbai 400037, Maharashtra, INDIA
E connect@thepencilapp.com
W www.thepencilapp.com

Author biography

Clearly, I am a writer, and my dream was to become a writer. I always wanted to be the center of attention to prove my success was something that I wanted to show the world that I love and like to do at home for a living because I will never be able to do anything else but write to type and to become popular, hoping and praying that an excellent achievement will come my way if that comes to me in the future to meet someone to turn my writing into something big, hoping others will see me as an author and hoping to believe someone will see me as a popular woman. Psalms 27:2 When the wicked advance against me to devour me, it is my enemies and my foes who will stumble and fall.

CONTENTS

1. Yellow Pussy Flower

OK, I feel relieved to know that paw really doesn't understand how I feel. He just wants to fuck other bitches over my head and paw seems to not get it. I see he just seems to be confused about which woman he wants to date. Every time I text him, I get text ignored because of the bitch bm who scratched his car up. It's a damn shame. As I was posting on Snapchat about his crazy bm fucking up his car, it really irritated me that she scratched the fuck out of his car with big lines and wiggly fucking lines on the side of his two car doors. It's not that easy when you're dealing with a man like Paw, who has feelings for several women. I don't have time for him to be in my company if he's going to be all up in some other woman's face and not me. He can keep himself to himself. I'm not lonely, and it's my place to be alone without him because I can.

2. a gift it's how he acts

I was on Snapchat one day when I noticed Paw car was all scratched up and messed up on the side of his car door on Snapchat, and he was like, "Man with three emoji hands on the face," and I thought to myself, "I betcha a woman did it, and I bet it was his new bm who did it because ain't no man going to scratch up another man's car but a woman." I was just guessing, but I knew it was her. It wasn't a guess because it wasn't something I guessed about because I fucks with Paw and he always has some shit with him. I see things I don't like about him because I fuck with him because anyone should have the decency to know and understand that his bm did this shit and I was so fucking mad at this nigga until it was a shame. Yes, his bm, yes, paw. I was like, "This bitch can't do the same thing as me." I was like, "This hoe ass bm needs to stop with this."

3. didn't mention his name

When I really saw those lines going across paw car, I was really not too happy about that because I knew I had to speak my peace about what was going on about what she did. and I didn't really appreciate what she did to my man car, so I said about her. I was on Snapchat and I didn't really care who knew who was going to know. I don't know if they found out who I was referring this to and what I said about Paw, but pretty much they should have known who I was talking about. I didn't even mention his name, they should have seen it on his Snapchat. I just didn't mention his name because it got too many messy folks out here, but it's just something I didn't want to say in his name because I think I didn't have to speak about his name because I thought it wasn't really anyone's business. even if they were aware of his Snapchat. I really didn't care.

4. snapchat

It was something I said about this stupid ass female on Snapchat. And for what she was mad for, because I don't see why she would be mad to take control. which is insane to me because I can't see myself trying to destroy a man's car because he doesn't seem to want her or is not trying to fool with her. I know Paw is more interested in me than in his new hoe ass bm because his bm was just a cake in the ass of a piece of cake to get. Because she has an ass behind her ass. I don't see what Paw was into her about because his bm ain't shit anyways and I'd rather be happy alone if he's going to be disrespectful like a slut and this shit doesn't have any meaning to them because he needs to leave this bitch who's a bitch. I'd rather Paw do it, and I hope he's willing to do the right thing by me so I can put this voodoo pussy on Paw. That's right, voodoo pussy.

5. scratched his car up

She scratched his car up and I was wondering what was on her mind and what she was thinking when she did this and why, because I really think she is an ass because I think this is something that she wanted because she is a crazy bitch. She wants to do crazy bs shit behind his back when he turns his back to do something with his car. She wants to scratch paw car all up before Father's Day, which is sad to do the smallest thing to hurt a man. She really needs to get her shit together because this is for the front and this ain't going to get her to the front stage, and this ain't going to get her to be doing the most out of nothing but trouble in her life. She thinks she's self-made, but I'm here to tell her she ain't self-made enough to be fucking up my friend car for nothing because paw hasn't done her anything but given her a piece of that pie, and she's mad for what? bm needs to go sit down and chill.

6. Things go wrong

That's why things go wrong for me and paw because he never wants to do the right thing by us. But he wants to be disrespectful. I just don't see why he doesn't want to take full action on his responsibility with me. Because if paw can lie down and have other children to make babies with other women and raise them, he should take care of me the same way he takes care of his bms. So what can he do for me? Just like that, child support can come out of his pocket to raise and take care of those children to give to his bms. I should get the same package if possible. And it's really sad that when things fall into place, he has to take on the big responsibilities over matters involving me. if he can not do this for me. If he can't do those things, then I don't need to be in a relationship with paw if he can't do those things priorities.

7. us privately

Paw needs to devise a strategy for making things right between us privately, because that's all we really have right now: friends with benefits and nothing more or less. Because I don't want to be with him at all because the shittiest thing he does is post his bm up on Facebook. I am not with that shit that he does because I'm still stuck with the girl who fucked his car up before this post with his other bm, and then after his car got fucked up by his other bm, she was mad about something he did because it could be the bm he posted on Facebook, but that's not the damn point, but why did the lady mess his car up? And why, poor thing had a baby for my friend Paw and now she realizes he's not investing in her love and perfection. She wants to be paw best friend, poor thing. I hope she finds some clarity on what she did to his car.

8. Bae's car door

I said something on snapchat about the problem with the scratches on the sides of his two car doors, front and back, which is what I saw on snapchat. I said, "Somebody put a big line scratch on the side of my bae's car door." If he had stopped messing with one of those hoes, maybe his car wouldn't have gotten fucked up. "Sad ass females out cha, tired ass hoes, that hoe needs to go to bed at that time of the night scratching up somebody else's car." That was the day after Father's Day, Sunday, June 19, 2022 at night time, but that happened on a Monday night after 1 or 2 am. That bitch should have been in bed by that time of night, watching paw damn baby. What mother in her right state of mind would do such a crazy thing to paw car? She needs her ass fucking whoop for that shit, fucking up that man's car like that. That baby she had for paw was more important to take care of than going to scratch her dad damn car up. Stupid hoe must be stopped. Oh, crazy ass.

9. more drama ensues

More drama ensues when this other bm creates a fictitious Instagram page message about Paw. I don't know why. I tell you, she is really starting some shit, I tell you, and then I wonder why she is so slow at making a fake page, thinking I didn't know that was her. The other bm, she was really a pain in the ass for doing this, and I knew she was harassing me because every time I see her, she will always look at me and zoom by me in her car when I walk to the store or somewhere one day, and she will give me those crazy-ass wired eyes passing by. And she will come up to the cash register to close when she buys her toddler things like socks. When she did see me at the store, what really took place was when she started some shit at the store with me. This bitch is crazy and a slow-ass fuck, but I hope she gets her mind right.

10. she stalks me

She stalks me everywhere I go, and everything I know she says she's going to do is beat me, but if the bitch wore a chip on her shoulders where her head is, her eyes would fucking see, and this bitch wouldn't say anything to me about beating me, but I'm going to show that hoe who's the woman boss, bitch, in this pussy paw be in, so she might want to wipe her shoes down. Because bitch, I'm coming for that ass, Mr. or Miss Post Bitch Man, he/she bm that paw has for a bm looking fucking man, dick pussy nigga, that hoe better stay in line or I'ma get that hoe in line myself. I believe that hoe had too much dick in her mouth from paw dick. Yes, paw dick, bitch suck. And she had better suck that dick hard. because my pussy isn't leaving this nigga side. She says she's sucking that dickey. She longs for her pussy licks. Hoe wants her dick sucked.

11. why the lies

Why the lies about I sucked your pussy? This girl lied to me, and to me, and on me. I will tell what she said. I never sucked this bitch pussy, never, and then she was going to turn around and say "I'm fucking paw bm lee lee" and know who in the fuck is Lee Lee, who has a pregnant bm baby by his cousin. She said she was pregnant by him again. Paw never had or got Lee Lee preg, his cousin. From my understanding, he had another fucking baby. Oh, dumbass quick, who says that kind of nonsense? Come and eat my pussy like you've been doing. This made me so mad that I had to text and call this girl more than once to clear my mind about what she had said to me. That girl had me heated and had me in my zone for once. Why lie to me about having eaten your pussy? This is not true. This girl must've fantasized about wanting me to eat her pussy because not this way.

12. why call me a bitch

For what reason, I don't know. She called me a bitch for no reason in the Instagram inbox. I thought I was going to scare the bitch away by calling the police on her the last time. I saw her at Supermarket Foods, but she has to put up a show for all this shit that she had to say to me what she had to say in my Instagram messages. What she could have said on her real page I had to ask her why she was calling me a bitch. I felt there was no need for her to be in my inbox all behind paw who makes babies on her for other women, but she claims I'm always stupid and slow for paw. but it's sad that she has to feel the way she feels about me. I will never be slow behind a man like Paw, who wants a threesome with me and other women. Everything she speaks of is a copycat. She enjoys imitating the cat with everything I do with paw. She pretended to be a shopping fake bm spirit wife.

13. copycat

So she felt that I was slow fucking with paw, so why would she think so slow of herself? Basically, I'm not the slow one like she is. But Shonta ran out of paw family because Paw had another baby with another woman. So that's why she left her family, but instead shonta wants to make play videos with paw on Facebook. and not come back into the paw family. What do you think I'm slow? I wouldn't come back either. I've never been in a nigga family. That's the reason why I'm not joining the Paw family. Paw enjoys fucking other women and having children. bitch I have not been in this man's family at all. So how come I'm slow? I ain't taking care of a man that doesn't take care of me, that makes babies for other people like paw bms. I ain't helping shit and I ain't going around paw families for shit. It ain't my responsibility to check to see if the paw family is straight.

14. Been-that big___bee_

Why are you still worried about me talking to paw? I told her everything she needed to know about me and Paw. Girl, I do not want to be with your baby daddy. I am not in a relationship like she is. I am not joining his family and taking care of his children like shonta is taking care of all of their children by paw bms. I am a single woman and am always going to stay single and away from paw family and others. Yep, bitchy. paw all up in my pussy, laying down with me. Because if she were any kind of woman, she wouldn't be behind a fake page to tell me some shit like this about paw. She ain't no real woman, anyway. She isn't showing herself on her real page to tell me about Paw. Does she need any more questions, bitch? I said to her, "Because me and Paw have been fucking for 10 years, and paw ain't going nowhere. So Shonta was the big_bee_instagram page, but the big bee was that ass Instagram big bitch instead of the big bee Instagram.

15. Lee Lee

No, Lee Lee is not expecting a paw. No, I know, but this is how it all began. He wants to give his dick away to crazy gravy-site girls that go off and mistreat him to have babies with other niggas, but he so says that's what he wants. Other women would dog him out and make babies on him for other men, but this is how it all started. I called her back to let her know the answer. I rang her inbox to let her know that I knew that it was her. LaShonta says, "You're going to be stupid forever." She continues, "You know Lee Lee," is expecting paw, huh? "You fucking her as well?" Fuck you, girl, with your slow fucking ass. paw don't want you hoe, I said, bitch. I could never be stupid, and Paw can fuck whoever he wants. Who the fuck is Lee Lee? bitch, you don't know anything about me to be fucking any girls. bitch I don't fuck girls, I don't like girls, and whoever is lee lee, I'm not fucking no lee lee.

16. dumb cuckoo

So like she said, Lee Lee is pregnant for paw and I'm going to forever be stupid. LaShonta is going to be a slow, dumb cuckoo hoe for the rest of her life as well. I could never be a slow bitch. She was dumb and cuckooed for messing with paw. No, she's a fucking slow bitch, I told her, but that's all that trash mouth she always has in her mouth, trash-talking shit. I hope LaShonta went and washed and cleaned her mouth out because of all that filthy shit she said, "I don't give a fuck who paw gets pregnant." I don't give a fuck if Lee Lee is pregnant, or whoever else is pregnant. "Bitch, really think I care about who's getting pregnant for paw?" Don't come to me with that nonsense. Trust and believe in me. I'm not a slow fucking paw. Paw don't think I'm a slow bitch when I'm fucking him. Emoji bursts out laughing because I'm fucking paw, my pussy is good to paw, and paw be moaning.

17. tie-down

and she laughed, "LaShonta." Her laugh felt like the fuck off her face. Not my laughter. She said paw doesn't want me, but my guess is as good as hers because I don't want him and that's why I'm single and that's why paw isn't single, paw in a relationship with me, that's why he keeps coming back for more and that's why I keep him running back for more because I got this pussy to tie-down on that dick, I got this dick all up in this pussy. This bitch is a psychotic depression hoe. This bitch needs to go get some fucking help because she needs it to take paw off her mind so she can stop worrying about who in the fuck paw messing with. "Roof", the dogging baby mother, I audio called that girl again. and she still didn't pick it up. She told me to stop calling her "ugly ass." I told that girl, you started it first with your unattractive stink.

18. fucking everything

LaShonta said, "Paw fucking everything," and everything is her. She will tell me when the last time I went to the doctor. I believe it's none of her business. She said all I do is suck paw dick. He ain't fucking me. But that's crazy. Because all me and paw do is fuck the night away. That girl was lame and mentally disturb. I asked her when the last time she went to the doctor. I told her I saw her post on Facebook on paw page. I got called "big mast hoe," which means she's the big mast hoe. I said, and she said, "Go take a bath in that little house, you big mast hoe." She didn't have to worry about me because I stay taking a bath all the time. Because I could never be a mast hoe, then she is a mast hoe. She was going to ask me, "why you on his page?" am beat you hoe. I can slap the fuck out of this girl for calling me out by my name. " What's up with all the cussing? She acts like a kindergarten child instead of a grown wo-man ass. If she wants to be a kindergarten adult, she should stay that way because she has to learn by herself.

19. sucking it

She sucked his dick. She said I sucked his dick too because she must be sucking it. That's why she asked if I was sucking his dick. She can't stop saying my name to paw, and they got the rest of his fe-male friends to jump on instead of me about this shit. Go get that girl who scratched his car, not me. I don't have time for the drama other than for her to start some mess. I hope she grows up and sees the light and true colors that paw really enjoys me. He wants to come with me, and she needs to understand that's what he wants to come with me. And be with me because he can't be too happy with her. Because he always comes running back to my pussy where he is satisfied and happy. paw is not happy with LaShonta. paw just doesn't get it right now. He doesn't see why he can't fuck with me because he loves my pussy better than LaShonta. I know paw will not be satisfied with just messing with her without me. I know this for a fact. So she needs to get over it and let it go.

20. I call the police

She asked for this call because she inboxed me from her real page and LaShonta wanted to pick on me about buying my book. She said can she buy a book. I spoke to one of my psychics, Linda. She said, "I see that she has issues." What she means by that is she's not the right person. Dear, she is very evil and she felt like if she was to ask you about the book, she felt like you wouldn't give her an answer or either let her buy it. That's how she felt. She felt like she wasn't going to get anywhere, especially since she acted that way with you. She's very jealous of you. I was like, she said the ugliest things to me on my Instagram. Why did she feel she had to say such things to me and everything was about how I'm still fucking paw? She asked me, "Can she buy a book first?" "What was the problem with asking me to buy my book?", and Linda told me, and I told Linda what she did in my inbox on her real page. I called the police on her ass for threatening and harassing me.

21. It's to small

That's why I said, in her dirty-ass apartment, which was a rundown trash apartment, everything would be a lie about what she said about me. I had to go take a bath out of her mouth. That's because she has to go take a bath with her stinky old puss. She doesn't have to worry about me. I love taking showers because that's something she doesn't love to do in hell. I'm clean in heaven. What about her because she is so fucking evil? She is truly evil. I know, some may be called evil, but not like her evil, as she is really evil. For real, I'm good and she's evil, so she may want to get ready for hell because. That's where God is going to call her in hell for picking on me. and for being evil. I hope she reaps what she sows down in hell. Because it's hot as hell down in hell and that bitch ain't going to be able to receive cold air in hell, I hope she has coldhearted days in hell when she leaves to go down. I am not playing, she is really evil. It's no lie.

22. some may call people evil

As I said, some may call people "evil." That's because they are going to heaven. I spoke to Rebecca Rossi. She was telling me that Lee Lee, yes, She is evil and her aura is full of negativity. But I'll get to that part about Lee Lee being evil soon. This means that both wo-men are ungodly. They are both not religious. They both worshipped Lucifer in hell, but in other words, Lucifer was a Christian. Before God sent him down to hell and made his own hell, some people don't understand that there are a lot of evil people in this world. and some may not believe someone that's close to them, like a family member or friend, is evil. Will never know until find out. Evil people are so messy, just like us real Christians. and some of our fake Christian pranks. I heard Dreezy on one of her albums. She said I'm not religious. I heard she was evil too, but I know she's evil too. It's common sense.

23. she said it's small

How is it small when she keeps sucking it? It can't be that small for her to keep sucking it up. She must be like to suck paw dick. She said it was too small. She said she's been sucking it up. Guess what? I don't care if she's been sucking it up, she said my man ate her ass. But bitch grammar ain't all shit and right. She should go improve her grammar. I told the thing to keep sucking its stink hoe. "Every time she sucks it, I'm tasting her pussy with my broke dumb ass," she explained. I could never be broke and dumbass, but she is such an evil bitch. One thing I could never taste was her pussy on his dick because he would never let me taste that dick anyway. I'm always fucking that dick, not sucking that dick. By the way, her pussy ain't on his dick because my pussy stays on top of his dick but not in my mouth. Other than that, she likes to keep sucking his dick... ha ha ha ha!

24. she called me ugly

She called me an ugly ass. This is how she said it. Stop calling me with your ugly ass. She is ugly as hell too, with her ugly muffin-top stomach. We said some things before I blocked her from my social media on Instagram and after I called the cops on her because she said she was going to spit in my face if she saw me before all this and I was confused because I wasn't planning on fighting her. So why would she want to spit in my face? And I felt like she threatened my life by saying she was going to spit in my face. So she started all this trouble between us first. I didn't say anything to her but told her to stay away from me and the mess and drama she had with me and what grudge she had against me. I don't know for what because her first answer was "bitch, are you still fucking paw?" That was her first answer to asking me these questions.

25. ungodly evil

Yes, she is ungodly because I know that she admitted that she was evil. Linda herself admitted that she was evil. She is ungodly because she doesn't like to worship the man up above in the blue sky with the white clouds, but to me, she lied about being ungodly. Instead of worshipping God up above, she wants to be fully into Lucifer in hell. I told that girl to brush her teeth after she finished sucking paw dick. She said, "I'm living off the first of the month check, but damn, at least my bills get paid for." Why pick a mess when she's living off hell checks? and say things in one way and play like herself and then Lee Lee in the inbox. At least my pussy ain't sore in hell like her. That wasn't Lee Lee's paw cousin in the inbox. It was her. Other than like her, my pussy clean up in heaven and on earth. She goes and says, "Bitch, come eat my pussy like you been doing ugly slow like that was Lee saying it." Now, I'm not as ugly and slow in heaven as she is. She's puking and throwing up in hell with her ugly ass.

26. I don't have a job

She said, "I don't have a job." It seems to me I have never seen her with a job besides the one bedroom she sleeps in with all those different baby daddy children whose dads were in special aid like that chicken neck nigga girlfriend paw has for having issues skank. She said I'm an ugly slow hoe, but she's not doing right at home, and she's not making it bitchy with those ugly ass braids and fake lenses. She claimed I didn't have a job, but she has no right to say that. Which energy is a fake strong energy, which is a bitch that doesn't have any strong energy. With that strong slow energy, it doesn't make any sense to have a newborn baby for paw again. Yes, Paw had another child with her on me, and this is his second child with her. " I'm so glad I'm single and don't have to help paw, and now paw officially has 11 children by different bms. Most likely, Paw needs to help me, not me help him. Thanks!

27. I could never be slow

I could never be slow for a man like paw, and he isn't my cup of tea anyway, and his dick ain't gold to me, so why waste my time on a man like paw that doesn't want a life with me and doesn't want to give me anything, and paw has too many kids anyway, and then he has the authority to ask for $100 to $50. He stated that I could at the very least give him $100 to cashapp him. Paw is insane to think I'm going to give him money to spend when all I've given him is my treasure gold for many years and he's never given me a dime to spend for my personal needs, and he thinks I'm going to give him everything in my life and give him the fucking world and every piece of my heart and soul and everything paw fucking needs so he can rob me of my fucking joy of happiness and take my money and run with it with his fucking feelings come first. No, my feelings come first. I would never give the devil my money to go run off and spend on his family. No way, baby, never.

28. he is at her house

Paw isn't at her house every damn day. She has no idea where he is. So, how is paw at her house when he is at mine? I had to tell her to stop making fake pages to get to me so she could give me a piece of her mind. I told her to stop sexually harassing me in my inbox. I had to ask her who she calling "ugly stinkmouth bitch" and "ugly muffin top." I could never be broke. Don't play with me. I don't like girls because she has it to say I like girls. I've never eaten pussy and will never start. I will never eat pussy because I don't like pussy and will never do that or try to mess with girls. So why lie to me about liking girls? That's because she likes my pussy better than paw. That's why she was in my inbox lying because she wanted a piece of this pussy, but she will never get this pussy at all. He is at her house and he is at mine. case closed. Her man, my man. It's just that she has paw more than me. Our man.

29. thought I was pregnant

paw don't spend nearly enough time at her house for him to dump more kids on me. Damn, I could have almost had a damn baby for paw. For all the fucking we were doing in bed, I thought I was pregnant. But the intimacy wasn't all that tight enough to get a grip because It seems to me she is always in the way of our relationship, wanting to have intimacy with paw. But, as one of my readers pointed out, he had some sort of light that has greatly dimmed. When I questioned why he was having babies on me for other women, what was his purpose in getting by doing this to me? Who does he want? I don't want to hear that it's difficult for him to make decisions because he keeps saying other women on me. He lost his way because it seems to me he didn't lose his way. I don't understand why he can't just move on from this affair we have and just be with the other woman instead.

30. miss tula

Miss Tula, Hello, the spirit of confusion is upon him. (a question) Why? He did it because he needed it, and on top of that, it shows that someone he was close to who dabbled in the dark side of things didn't want to let him go. He also has a few family members, and they do not want him to move forward with good in life again. Why, you may ask? She asked me, continued, Because he has what they all do not have, and that is a positive spirit within him, but because he dwells amongst them, their negativity has become his comfort. This is why he makes nill decisions and his light has greatly dimmed. I found some more hidden secrets about his side, but I don't believe this because it's an excuse for him to dog me out the way he's doing to me right now and in the past. I do remember the past when he did karmically to me, and I was very upset with what he had done to me in the past.

31. hell and heaven

I'm not really sure if this is true or not, but I was told that paw like hell and heaven. So I never knew if a person like him liked both hell and heaven because I didn't know. I believe paw should like heaven the most instead of hell. Because paw would want to go up to be with God instead of hell. Because I just don't agree with hell because his bm is on the dark side. I truly believe I know where Miss Tula got this from, someone on the dark side who wouldn't let paw go. Linda was telling me that his bm, who recently had a newborn baby for paw on the month of July 25, paw said, "My queen has arrived," which was a paw baby who came into this world in 2022. That's his dark side, bm, because she worships the devil in hell. And as I can see, she was trying to get my attention by making a fake page to ask me about paw, trying to get close to being friendly.

32. it depends on both

It depends both on whether paw is going to hell or heaven. I asked a free question from Mark Morris where it says "Hello!" Feel free to share your feelings and date of birth, please! Mark asks me what's troubling you today, which leads me to ask a question about someone I truly want to know about. Since I heard his bm was ungodly, I wanted to know about paw. Is he good or evil? He said it all depends on the situation. It can be both good and evil. It all depends on who it's in relation to, and I was like, so you're saying paw could be good or evil? And he was saying to me, "He can be both good and evil." It all depends on the situation in which he is. I said, so he likes both? Mark was like, yes, and another thing he was saying was that I also felt a change in some of my areas. Especially there are those that have to do with your finances. I said, "Oh, really, OK."

33. treat me better

But besides the point, I told paw he had to treat me better than this throughout my text messages. I was like, "mann paw needs to treat me better than that the way he does, and he's outcha messing with these hoes." He is doing some fucked up shit by letting that hoe scratch his car up. If his hoe assaults me first, I'm gon na call the cops. That's all-paw wants to do is come over to have sex with me. and use me for sex, and play around with his bm behind my back. I sent paw a flirtation text message just to play with him. I'm not playing with paw as he plays with me because he plays too much, but I don't really care what paw does with his bm as long as I have my space from him and his family. I like peace and respect, away from them. I don't like people disrespecting me. I was not trying to be nice to him because he kept dogging me out, but I'll say what I said on the next page, chapter 34. With the flirtation, I told him.

34. flirtation

I told paw in my flirtation words, give me that dick, because if he doesn't, I'ma bite him when it gets here naw, if it doesn't come over naw, and there was no more flirtation anymore because I felt like it didn't have to continue on. I was not happy about a lot of things that paw was doing behind my back, which I found out in public from paw. I am over the trouble and karmic shit. I just don't like the expiration behind the bs. With all the things paw got going on, I don't have anything to do with it and I don't like being used by a man like paw. He didn't do anything for me, but his bm was trying to get close to me because she was interested in my career. Why try to say things to me that will ruin my life and career in the name of being a fake loyalty-friendly person? I don't like fake hope and faith. I want to live my life free from his bm and it just seems untrue to want to hang with me. Why does his bm want to hang with me to get close?

35. Are you gay

Because of all the fucking he does with women and his inability to relax, I had to ask paw if he is gay. Because paw fucks too many females, paw acts like he can't settle down with me. How many children does paw have if he has five different bms? Paw needs help. Paw needs to call Jesus because he really needs it. Paw needs to call the sex paramedic because paw really needs it. Paw going to fuck around with that bitch? The other chick is going to put him in jail. Paw had a baby for his other bm in 2021, the new one, and then paw turned around and had another baby for his other bm. He had two kids for her, and now paw has three with her now because he had the other two kids while we were having an affair together. and then paw disrespected me and called me out by my name. bitch what? "You called me gay?" he said.

36. calling me a bitch

I had to ask him who he thought he was calling a bitch. Because I'm not the one who paw thinks he's playing with. Stay in his place, nigga! He better shut his weak ass up and paw better stop playing with me. That's why I went out to eat at a date restaurant with another man. That's why I'm thinking about letting this sex thing we have for each other go. That's why I'm in a relationship with another man. But I wasn't with any man. I just told him that, and I felt I didn't do any wrong by calling him a bitch back. I deserve better and I was not fighting stones with stones with him. Because his spirit wife had won him back after all those years of teasing him. I just don't like the simple fact that he connives things so that he treats me so badly for his spirit wife. He was going to ask me after the facts, I told him, because since he is so damn hard-headed, you want to fuck, he said. I told paw Oh, he got jokes. Yea, let's fuck, ha ha ha.

37. fr he said

He said, "I'm fr." "I'm just kidding," I said. I'm never leaving. " Did he bring up Wym? I said to him, "I'm never going to stop fucking him and stop picking mess. Oh messy ass, paw is going to tell me, never tell me you got a nigga or nothing of that, because next time I'm gone, I told that nigga to leave right naw, I ain't going to miss him, baby, paw said. Oh yeah? OK, he wasn't hurting me at all. He said, "So that's dead." I told paw Yup, go, yea, dead, yup. He said OK. I instructed him to not come creeping up to my door when I blocked him out and left him to his hoes. That's where he wants to be. bm with his hoes. He's going to tell me to block him and we'll never talk again. Good. That's what he wants me to do. Block him so we'll never see each other fucking again. Leave, bitch, because paw has been fucking other hoes. bye bitch, Go be with those stank hoes just like your stank ass. I said all this to him because he truly pissed me off to the max. That's why I called him "stank." No meaning, he is not a stank man because he is a very clean person.

38. cold-hearted at times

Paw can be harsh and cold-hearted at times, so what does that mean I want to fuck? Don't try to play me like that's all I like to do. Don't disrespect me, nigga. Don't knock at my back door anymore. My boyfriend is going to be here. I was just giving him the heads-up. Naw bye! Stay away from my house and that fuck word, which he can't say in a single way. Because he is so mean and disrespectful, I don't want to fuck with him. And then he makes me mean to him back because I don't like that. He said, "I want to play with him." I was like, " OK, bye." This is not about playing with him. Okay, he just takes me the wrong way about things he doesn't understand. but he will never get it and will never understand sometimes. I am thinking he is slow when it comes down to his women and his spirit wife. I said "boy fuck you shit" because that's what it is. Fuck him. He goes on to say, "Remember that." Hey, remember my ass nigga? "

39. OK goodbye

I had to inform paw that he was still leaving me with this question. He's going to tell me goodbye when I should be telling him goodbye and good night. OK, goodbye. He said, "I'll never text you again." No, don't ever text me again. OK, Paw, are you still leaving me? So what is he going to say to me? Man, you said what you said and fuckin' other muthafucks. What muthafucks? I ain't fuckin' other muthafucks. Which is a goddamn lie, why is he worried? I deserve to be happy with someone else anyway because he has a spirit wife. I was before her anyway, just because she won paw publicly and I just couldn't get the facebook posts like he did with his other bms from his past. He posted all his bms from the past and not me, but though he finally stopped and started settling down with his other spirit wife. But the answer is that he feels comfortable with me, but the thing is, if he feels comfortable with me, then where is my money from him?

40. loyal and faithful

He's going to tell me, man, ain't you said what you said and fuckin' other muthafuck's. I had to tell paw he was trippin' fuckin' other muthafuck's. Don't play with me. I don't fuck other people, and I don't fuck other muthafucks. I am very loyal and faithful and if he or anybody sees me make any posts on social media or hears anything from anyone, it's because paw is with his bm and I'm single. I don't have anyone to be fuckin' with others. That's because he is insecure and unfaithful to me, and I'm single, and how could I be fuckin' other muthafucks when I'm a faith-based relationship person? I don't cheat. I was like and said, "Let me fuck him." That's what I told him. " And paw was like, "I didn't want to fuck last night, so no goodbye." And I was like, "He acted like he didn't want to fuck." Then he was like OK, and I was like OK, my ass.

41. No threesome

I had to let him in on something about to check his childish hoe. I had to let paw know to please check his childish hoes. He's got bitches checking me because they've gotten strong liking each other and I can't come in between. paw is a pain in the ass because for what I am saying, paw says, "say," and I said, "what?" He is going to tell me to stop texting numbers that text me? I told him to stop texting numbers. He said that if I text, I don't text them, and wyd? I told him no, that he should tell his bm to stop creating fake pages, and why not? paw asked me if I was trying to ride this. I was like yes, I guess, and paw was like fr, and I said ok, and paw asked me again if he was waiting to have a threesome tonight. We can? He asked, "I'd never had a threesome with paw and never will," and I was like, "with who? I was just curious to see not to say I liked her. I told him to let me see a picture first. and he was like, "Nevermind," and I told him, "No, no threesome."

42. Facebook messenger

I ask paw can he do that thing one day again like he did before? I love him, big baby. He went to say his goodbyes. Don't say goodbye. I should be telling him bye because he doesn't have the right to tell me bye. I'm the woman. He's the man. He should stay in a man's place. I told him to come get this pussy and give me that dick. Yo, ya, the bitch is in the inbox, me! Look in his Facebook messenger. He likes to call me a bitch once he gets mad sometimes. Let's go to Atlanta, Georgia, and California one day privately, just me and him alone. I had asked him this question. I asked him if he wanted to fuck because that's all he really wants to do is fuck and asking him to go to the city ain't going to happen. That's going one out the other ear for this man, but it wasn't anything serious. I asked him anyway. I didn't want paw anyway. I don't see us going any further to make something happen, but just the same to keep it going affair.

43. I am not a bitch

I will never allow a man to call me a bitch. especially a man-like paw after he wanted to see my pussy. Everything was OK, and then, before that, paw wanted to have a threesome tonight. "Can we do that?" he inquired. "He'll see if he brings her," he said. I told paw no, because, as I previously stated, I don't need him to disrespect me. I already went through too much with him anyways. I don't need the drainage, and he goes, "Wow, now I said, what's up with the wow?" I don't need all this for what he asked me to do. It's not a wow and it's not a big deal. He should need to go ask his spirit wife bm to have a threesome with him. He could have a threesome with whoever he wanted, but not with me, hun. I asked him why he was starting a drama. I'll wait until he gets here by himself. I said, "Don't bring no girl over here because I'm going to call the cops," and he was like, "OK," and things are always OK with him. I told paw that I would wait until he arrived before he got here.

44. aye

He aye told me and was waiting for something for me to do with him, and he asked me to unlock that door, and I was ready when he was ready to make that piece happen for us. Wyd Dickey? I was asking, but he was always coming back to get this pussy, so I took a chance to text him in his free time while he wasn't with me. One day I was wishing we could go to Disney World, just me and paw, privately, just the two of us lol, no pictures or none of that, with nobody knowing but me and paw, so we could fuck on a vacation by ourselves with no one around but me and him. We need to go on a Disney World romantic trip. No family allowed, baby, and it doesn't have to be serious. Just think about it. It would be fun. Nobody knows us in Orlando, Florida, in Disney World, like our hometown, and we can come back the same way we did. That's it. I don't know what he said. I was like, "What did I say?" because he gave me the emoji eyes.

45. why ask me again

One thing about me I don't give up on repeated answers. I told him to come stick me in my pussy like he did that night, and why did he ask for a threesome again? Why was this repeated? He must have wanted to see that hoe go to jail and he was like, with what hoe? Lmao, I told him to stop asking for a threesome. I told him to stop playing with me before I fuck his hoe up. He wanted to have a threesome with me. So he lmao paw again, and there he goes with the OK, as if it's always OK with him when it's never an OK. I had to put him in his place. He says, "Man, why am I fussing? He is hard-headed and doesn't listen. " His head seems to be hard-headed because he started the shit. He's not going to ask any more questions. "That's nonsense, I said," he explained, "but I'm supposed to please him, right?" He just wanted to try something, but this is something he shouldn't try with us. I told him he live for the drama with hoes.

46. romantic trip

I repeatedly asked him if he wanted to go to Disney World in Orlando, Florida in 2022. It was said through text, but I really did say that already. I legally stated that he didn't want to fuck, so he said goodbye for what? Really funny, ha ha ha. Since Beyonce wants to say church girl song lyrics, drop it like a thotty, drop it like a thotty. I could never be the second woman in paw life, like in supernatural life. Daniel Adams said Beyonce's Church Girl Song Is All Kinds of Wrong! Paw should not begin with me, not at all. I mean, play with me if he wants, He started messing and damming with those thotties on me, and this could never happen. I wouldn't even let this happen. This threesome could never happen. No, and it was no. He said, "Man, good night." He was coming, but I then pmo, which means I project management officed him. He had better stop playing with me. No, fuck no, that's not something to please him, no.

47. pleasing him

Pleasing him is all he requires, and he doesn't need to require another third bag in the bed to do this work because I'm a whole lot of woman for him, so why does he require a threesome to please him when I'm his pleaser to please that ass? Okay is his favorite word. Who else's favorite word is okay? At that point, I said to him, "I don't want another bitch in bed." He said, "Well ok," and I said, "If I'm not pleasing him, then move the fuck on." Oh yea, he said ok again, and if he thinks another bitch is going to please him by having a threesome with us, what the fuck is he coming over to me for? "Get out of here, boy," I yelled, "because what do I care about a hoe fucking him in front of me?" I said. I had to go tell paw to go sit down through a text message. I need to replace him for another man, so I can leave his ass for good. And speaking of what I said, I told paw he's got a mom, two grandmas, sisters, and daughters.

48. i'm not his bitch

Respect me, baby. I'm not your bitch, I'm not his bitch or threesome. ' Call his mom a bitch,' Paw said, "OK, ha ha! I told paw to have respect for me just like his women in his family. And most likely, I was saying to paw that just like he has respect for his mom, sisters, grandmas, and daughters, he mostly needs to have respect for me, just like his mom, and like I said when I spoke on his mom to him, intentionally paw word was OK, ha! I was starting to not like him anymore. He said, "Imma go then." I told him, "Well go then, and don't come back to fuck." Fuck that. If he is going to disrespect my body and make me feel uncomfortable, he needs to pay for my pussy. He needs to apologize for this threesome. He wants I believe he owes me an apology for disrespecting my body language. How can he tell me that my pussy isn't good enough without pleasing him with another woman.

49. isn't satisfied

When his dick can't even get up sometimes, and I'm the one who isn't satisfied here and pleased enough, and he wants to talk about another stink hoe bitch? I'm not pleased with what's going on with what he said about what he is thinking in his mind. Everything he then said was all wrong. I told this man paw bitch, my pussy is not weak, don't be calling other trifling ass hoes power, what the fucks is wrong with this bitch, don't play with me with his pussy ass hoes, I have never eaten anybody's pussy, I will never eat anybody's pussy in my entire life. I told paw that if he wants to go fuck others, he should do so without me. Paw is going to ask me if I'm awake. I know paw is always picking up a mess with me. I had to ask him, why? "Nevermind," Paw says, "I told him not to ask if I'm awake." If it's a nevermind, he's going to say, "OK, I won't."

50. OK I won't

It's always about OK but never really serious about anything we go through with each other. I told him, "Don't play with me." OK, he said, "I won't. This is another I won't. I had to tell him he had better straighten up his energy better than that. What does he always mean to ask me? What exactly do I mean? I told him to stop his negative thinking. He wanted to fuck me with a female. I'm not his mind. I don't want to fuck females with paw. Well, he said, "Well, let's fuck then shit." He wanted to fuck me instead, and I was like, "Yea, whatever." Of course, nothing sha, he said ok, but boy was he getting on my nerves. I told him I missed him, and he said he missed me back. Does he miss me? And he was like, "I'll come back when something is right. Until then, I ain't coming. " And I was like, "He ain't going nowhere." He answered like I said, until he could do what he said, he was not coming. He will get over it and come by himself.

51. it is all a lie

It was all a lie. I told him to do whatever he wanted. Not a threesome, just the two of us. What does it mean? He told me what he wanted. I asked him, "Didn't he already do that?" I'm not sure. I said, "Give me a kiss, give me a kissy." So paw kept asking the questions and I wasn't responding to what he was saying but giving him the monkey's emoji and the eyes and he was like "yup." I told him he was a trip and he was going to tell me he was serious. Well, damn, I'm serious about this too, but not in the way paww was serious. Paww can't have his cake and eat it too. I'm serious too, but no and he was going to say no what? He was questioning me about what he shouldn't be questioning me about and what I didn't want him to do, but all he could do was fuck my pussy naw. I asked him to come get it and he was going to say, "I'm good until he does whatever he's gone to."

52. I'm good—I'm gone

But paw wanted to come and do whatever he wanted, so he went, but that's not to say he's not coming right now or at the moment to fuck with me, so he'd have to fuckin go then and don't come back because that doesn't make any fuckin sense over something like that, which is pitiful. He wants to say OK bye, and I said, God bless him, and he's going to say bye for good. Just let it be bye for good because I shouldn't waste my time on him when I could be sitting around doing graceful things with my life instead of having sex. I told paw, Okay, that's enough. Don't text me no more then. He thinks it's a joke and what I get from him is a bye. I asked the cow how old he is now and he never answered. I know paw is 28 years old, so he has his birthday on October 29 and his year of birth is 1993, but I just knew his age was something like that because I just asked him and wanted to know. That's all because I knew and I wanted him to tell me himself.

53. the age didn't matter

Age didn't matter in the conversation of text messages. It was just something to hold in a conversation to ask about something to talk about. Nothing means more to me than anything serious to ask about, because he's getting much older and I just remember when I first meant him. He was really stuck up, and he was 22 or 23 years old when I meant him, but he was alright at the beginning until I found out how bad of a person he was, and paw turned out to be the worst and worst man ever to mess with, and besides the point, I don't know what he was mad at, but he needed to stop it. And his first word was, "aye!", and I was like, "What?" and paw said, "What?" And I replied, "Aye?" and he said, "Wyd?" I told him I was going to get up, take a shower, and go to the store this morning, and he said, "Well, I'll catch you later." What did he mean by "catch me later?" Later, he said to me, "Who is he playing with, sir?" I had to see who Sir was playing with, huh?

54. don't handle me

I had to tell paw that he shouldn't be fucking with me like that and handling me the way he did. I had to inform paw of his problem. He was not acting like this last month, boo. bm is treating me wrongly by harassing me on Instagram again. Why is he so fucking evil? paw for Satan, the Devil. I said to give me that dick, Paw. He was going to give me the eyes and I gave him the emoji back face-rolling and he asked this what shit question and I told him nothing because it was something he didn't need to know. I said, "Give me kissy, give me kissy paw again." When can we have the sleepover again? " I sent paw a heart to him. I'm going to find myself a full-time Christian man. Paw is bad, evil guy. I don't want a half-evil, half-good man. I'm tired of paw. I'm tired of paw and he's going to say, "Okay, everything is OK with paw." He was aggravating me, and yes, I told him this. Why is he letting this hoe ass star comment on his shit and I can't? nigga got me fucked up.

55. I'm hot and horny

I'm hot and horny. I discovered one that I like. All the other dildos I didn't like, so I chose the pink one. Paw's question about the size of his dick was not about the size of his dick. Paw is not a size 7, but rather a size 10. He is a winner, but besides that, I can't wait to fuck paw again. I've been wanting to do it again. I've been wanting to fuck him lately again. I had to cuss him out once again. Bitch, paw has no power. He is weak. Anything he sticks his dick in those hoes' pussies, he calls bm hoes. They are both hoes. Fuck him and his trick kids, bitch. I had to tell paw that he could never ask me for $50 to $100 again in his life. I never gave him money anyway. I will never support his hoe-ass kids' family. I am a book publisher and I will never help him to support him and his family. Paw doesn't do anything for me anyway. He will never take care of his kids with my money in the future.

56. coming through

paw wants to come through quickly. He said he was coming through J-Town. That's what he said. I told him to just come. I'm tired. He was saying OK in texts. I was telling him that my body hurt right now, and so he said, "Don't come." I told him he had to come and give me a piece of that dick. I told him he could come over, and he was going to tell me, "Not if my body hurts." He didn't want to hurt me. " It's good, he said. I said, "He can or he doesn't want to come?" He said, "I'll be right quick." Do I have a rubber? " I said yea and paw wanted to see me oil that ass right now, and he said I'm about to pull up, I don't have any oil, I haven't bought it yet, and I told him his energy was not good, he was going to tell me he got me next time, and I said yea ok, I wanted to fuck again and try again, hoping things would be better for our sex when it happened again. When can we fuck again, I wonder? Bite bite bite bite.

57. spirit wife

I asked paw why he didn't tell me about his spirit wife, bm. Why didn't he tell me that his bm was his wife instead of me having to go through those emotional problems with him? This man never gives me the satisfaction of guaranteed answers back at all or the money back and guarantee out of his pocket, but I don't care if he does not answer or not. and I ask when he'll be here to get some? and he said, "Wyd?" I told him I was in bed. I told him I was busy today and he was like "aww" and I was saying "OK" and I told him I didn't want him to do something and he asked me why not? I told him I'm not doing it anymore. He said ok, and I asked paw how his day was today. And he said "good," and I told him, "that's good, good night," and he said "night." I told him I really did want to have him, but oh well, bite, when is he coming? " sex?

58. f_with_something_

She made another fake page, the real one, and oh really, the real one. Paw bm made another fake page. And I'm guessing she'll make another one just to mess with me again. So let me say what she said. Y'all still talk to paw, and in other words, in my voice, why is she wanting to know for what and is it really that serious for her to know that his spirit wife, paw bm, and this is what I said, why is she coming to me asking me these questions? It's not no y'all. It's the other girl, not me. Go see her instead of me. She's the one who had a baby for him? paw, yes, Go ask her that question and stop harassing me about this. To bother me about this, she must really like his dick. Why won't she just leave me alone about this? This is getting ridiculous over some man paw. She gave me the wow emoji face. She called me several times after that, but I refused. I was not having it with her phone calls over instagram and all that calling to get close. paw bm was calling me.

59. the real_one

After all the messages the real_one had sent me through messages, I looked over to her page, which was paw bm. She sent me a follow with a fake page. I never confirmed her follow because I didn't believe that it needed to be confirmed. I was not looking to be her best friend or sister's support, and I got and read from a reader who said something about her, and I knew it was her because she called me. The audio call started. I missed an audio call that had started about one call, I believe it was her, and the audio call had ended and it asked to call back, and shonta said hey, call me back, and I called her back. The audio call ended and I asked her, "You said call, why didn't you answer? That's what I said to her. She asked me who I was. She knew who I was. She was just playing dumb, and she was going to ask me if I still talked to catfish.

60. Shelta's voice

I said no, about when she asked about my ex-catfish, and she asked me who I talked to. Can we date? Why would I want to go on a date with her if I didn't like her in that way? I don't like girls. She was playing games and inboxing me on Instagram. BM: Shonta, the spirit wife paw girlfriend. The reader was saying something about the fake page she was making. I'm going to get into it right now. The voice of Shelta, the psychic reader, said for a visiting woman like me to ask a question, say hello! The fact that you're reading this means you are ready to change your life. Let me be your guide on this journey of transformation. Ask your most burning question, will you? Honey, what's bothering you today? So, say, I had to send myself to the voice of Shelta to ask my question. Hello? I have a question to ask? And she was like, "Yes, dear, ask your question," and I said, "OK, will she try to make another page to reach me again."

61. the reader

The voice of Shelta didn't want to give me an answer to the question I asked her about if she was going to make another fake page again. I don't know why she didn't tell me. I'm not sure why Shelta didn't tell me about what I asked her about whether she was going to make a fake again. So I do believe Shelta was lying to me that she didn't want to tell me if she was going to do it again, but she was saying to me, "Dear, I want to help you, but you have to understand that I feel people's energy and I can't tell you these details." I was OK. I don't understand. What is people's energy? Shelta was like a different sweet. I told Shelta, "Hun, I don't understand anything you are saying because there shouldn't be any people energy in this reading. Well, can I ask a different question since you didn't give me a free question." I was thinking to myself, "What does she mean about other people's energy? Something seems to not sound right. Yes, it was paw bm who created the fake page. Yes, I'm still on him.

62. Leo Alvarez

The other psychic was saying that the reading was paw bm was going to make another fake page and that's what I wanted to start with. I asked since the voice of Shelta didn't want to tell me about the fake page. Shelta said she feels people's energy. and all I know is that I had to ask Leo Alvarez again. Greetings! It's not the time to give up! Let's find out the answers together! Please answer your question! He then answered the second question for me. Hello! How can I help you? What question brought you to me? and I said, "Hello, Can I ask a free question? Leo replied back to my message. Yes, of course. What is it that concerns you? I asked that same question that I asked the voice of Shelta, and Leo said, "Let's see what the connection between your auras shows." I said OK. Leo said, "Spirits tell me that yes, she'll probably create new pages to contact you. It's stuck in her head. She thinks it's very important. "

63. emma brown

Emma Brown: Hi, this is Emma! My dear, I'm here for you, to help you, to share my experience and positive vibe! Let's start! Hello, how are you? " Hello, may I begin? Emma, sure dear! I said, "What is her reason for making a fake page again? So I had to block her because she said to call her, and I was curious as to why she was trying to approach me. Emma said, "Thank you, let me see, and I said OK." Darling, the spirits say it's like she wants some justice from you. But I said it's funny because when I asked Mary Rose about paw bm, all this was said first about Mary Rose, that I needed to first support her, and then it came true that the fake page was made by paw bm. But before I get to that part, let me first get on about Emma's reading. Emma said, "But also the spirits see that she is interested in you and wants to get closer to you."

64. Justice

I asked Emma what kind of justice she wanted from me. What kind of interest? Emma. Most likely, she thinks that you did not act fairly towards her. She thinks that you have devalued her feelings. I asked if she was still interested, and Emma told me honey, If you are interested, then we can find out exactly what she thinks about you and what interest she has in you on our reading. But though paw bm disrespected me and I'm not having this conversation with her later, why would I want a conversation with a person like her where her baby daddy dogs me out and she tries to find a way to get close to me? It was never an option for us to get close. There will never be an opportunity for us to get close. I don't want this option from her at all and I will never find a place in my heart to ever make us best friends. I truly do not agree with this criticism bm girlfriend paw has. She can just leave me alone with the harassing fake pages.

65. There is no cement soul

There is no cement soul sister. I wasn't having it, and when I finally got to Mary about the questions and answers, Mary's inbox said, "Hello and thank you, that you chose me as your expert. Hello, dear. How can I help you? And I said, "Hey, can I ask a question?" She was saying, "Yes, honey! What exactly do you want to know? I was telling her paw bm spirit wife and I feel like she's being very disrespectful towards me and I want to know what's going on with her and why? Mary said, but you don't have a relationship with her, right? I said, "No," and Mary said, "Okay, write me please your name and DOB! Also, her birth! I said ok, and I did, but I was not sure of her birth, but she was 28 years old. OK, I mean, a year, I didn't know the year of her birth, but OK, and she said thanks for the information. I'm checking your question! Mary got to the question that was answered. OK, dear.

66. behavior reasons

Her reason for her behavior can be difficulties at work or with family! And also, I see you have special feelings for her! and I see that you want to make her feel better! I see you have the type of compatibility that really cements the relationship for a long time. It is a timeless element that holds you together even when your views and interests change. Also, you still have an emotional connection with her! I see that for you, it is hard to understand her feelings. I told Mary she doesn't act as if she likes me. Mary told me, "Yes, but I see that you have a chance to be more close to her and support her! and I see that you need to reveal her feelings to you! And if you wish that, you need to take certain important steps! I ask if she will try to talk to me soon. Mary said I could also use a discount for reading! I said OK, and after the free reading,

67. discount reading

I was sent a discount to start another reading with Mary. She said, firstly, you need to do the first step with her! and I will show that to you in my personal session. And I said, "Okay, I'm ready." Mary once again was saying to me, "Okay, so in this situation, firstly you need to support her! because she is having a difficult time now! So now I will give you some tips on that! and I said, "Okay," I said. And she said,"And while you will support her, you will be close to her! Recognize the importance of this situation. Yes, you tried. It didn't work out, but it's very important that you did it! The feelings you are experiencing right now are very important. Sadness, loss of strength, all this is natural, but I am there and will help you. and I was wondering what kind of support I had to do for her. Mary says it is important for a person in a state of sadness to know that someone is nearby. Always remember this. I'm telling you exactly about that! It is not all, of course! and I said, "OK."

68. cement friendship

All this was about paw bm in this reading. I don't believe Mary Rose knows what she's talking about because I don't have a special feeling for her, not me, and this will never happen, and not for Shonta either. I'll never be able to hold a cement friendship rock together like Sister's, and I'll never want to see her get better in the first place, and I won't make her feel better either. Mary Rose was saying, "I know how to hold a cement forever friendship with someone as a sister. She's not my blood sister. Mary was talking about best friends but not her because she will never get this reward from me because someone else will before her and probably never with someone else either because I don't have any friends because people are full of drama for me. I will finish with more of what Mary Rose said about this cement friendship I have in me that Shonta can't get from me because this is not true at all.

69. depression problem

And about the reading, because I ain't done yet and this is more of where it came from. Mary said, "I am certain that everything I know comes from her for sure. more readings on part of the message Mary was saying, be there. Even if at the moment, the person refuses your help, Be there or nearby so that your friend always knows that if she needs help, she has someone to turn to. The support of loved ones for people with depression is very important, so if possible, do not ignore your loved one-whether it's asking for a walk, drinking tea together, or just talking on the phone, and Mary was like, just know I'm always here, and I was saying about paw bm to Mary, so you're saying she has a depression problem, and the reading went on, little depressions, yes, but it is not serious, and Mary said, "I was like, 'OK, is she looking to talk to me? And she answered back, "By making it clear that you are ready to be there in any situation, you are already providing support."

70. not providing support

If I'm not ready to be there in any situation, or by making it clear that I am ready, I am not already providing support, because I'm not doing any of these things. I'm not doing this. Sorry, not at all. This is not my responsibility. I have nothing to do with whatever this situation may be. This is not my duty to be providing help for paw wife, shonta. I am not their mother and supporter. I am not about to take care of two couples whose husbands I'm having an affair with. shonta was not first, I was. They are not married yet. They are together all the time, not with me, so they consider being husband and wife in the future. I know they are getting married in the future and it's not going to be with my help because I ain't helping. Excuse me, I'm not the provider to be helping paw and his bm while he uses me for sex to go off and marry her. Then I look like the slow, dumb person that I am. Anyway, I could never be that.

71. trying to use me

This will never happen. I know he's getting married to Shonta, and he thinks I'm going to stand around them while they get married and look like a fool. Why try to use me and make it seem so real that paw is a character. Paw wants to be a character user and can use me for money and sex. He can ask me for money and I can't. I am not a sugar mama. Paw is trying to scam me out of my money to give it to other women, but I will not let him treat me wrong. I will not tolerate this horrible mess that paw brings to me. No ma'am and no sir for the both of them. I do not play games. I know everything has come together as I knew, but I put two and two together and it became a match to what I thought I knew about them. Some psychic priest_omoighe told me something about a fought I had and fell out with someone in my past.

72. something suspicious

and it seems to me that it was some harassing person from my past who wanted to come into my life for support. At the same time, Paw is looking for support just like shonta. They are both saying the something, and it sounds suspicious that he is trying to use me for sex and money to get married to Shonta. I told paw, I am not your mother for you to be asking me for support. Some things seem to not be right because I sent him a message saying, as I told you the last time, I did not tell you to treat me like your mother. I told you, just like you support your mother, you support me with money, just like your mother. I am not your mother. You are not money and support. You understand? Stop disrespecting me for your wife. No, they are not married. This is what I told paw. Paw is always up to something when I really don't think anything is going on with him or why he has to be the way he is and does, so I never know what paw is up to. That's why I am very unhappy with where things are going for us.

73. book now

Rose was finishing off something about how, paw bm, a suffering person realizes how painful, and sometimes burdensome for others, her condition is and begins to close herself off from people. and tell me when you last talked to her? I see that she is focused more on her problems, but in some moments she thinks about you! I told Rose, it's been a while, a very long time, but there has been drama in between. Rose is going to ask me, "What can I do to help you? People experiencing a psychological breakdown are often unable to answer this question. However, your words will help someone who is going through a difficult period to listen to herself, to her desires. I will help you find your exit. If you see someone who is depressed, the best thing you can do is to help them get professional help. I understand you: it happened to her as well. The psychic had depression!

74. invisible woman

I just don't understand why paw thinks I have to support and stick by his side. I just don't understand why I have to be his mother to take care of him. If paw was wealthy, he would only have sex with me and take care of his other females, not me. If paw was a millionaire, he wouldn't give me a house and land for my pussycat. He wants me to give him money while he goes to spend time with his family and wife. I'm the invisible sex one while paw goes out to the stores with his bm wife while I sit at home looking stupid. Lord knows I'm not stupid or insane behind paw. Paw needs to get with the program. He may need to go find his invisible woman that's going to treat him with support because this is not a dead-end sex support in my way where he can just get money out of me.

75. breakdowns

So, paw bm breakdowns. Mary Rose again said, "The more and more freely she speaks about what torments her, the more she realizes that words resonate, the less helpless and lonely she feels. And gradually, the situation will begin to be perceived as not so hopeless. " I told Rose to speak to her. Yes, she said, I corrected it. I said, "OK, Rose. Be more close to her when she feels bad! As Rose said, try to reach her out! And try to learn these tips! So, thank you for taking the time to visit with me! I hope you will be fine! And I told Rose thanks for the reading. Rose said, "Hello, dear Anastacia! Recently, I rechecked your energy and I saw that this summer you will have interesting updates! It can also influence your immediate future. " So I can give you more information about the reading update! A 25% grab off for my next reading with Mary Rose was given to me, so I took the reading to see what Rose had to say because it wasn't important to me anyway, and also because she was telling me I could use the discount for my next reading with me! "

76. energy reading

The energy reading started by saying, "Hello my dear! You know, when I focused on your energy and noticed some progress in your love life! I see the situation with her is still difficult, but my spirituals guides told me what exactly you need to do now! So when you are ready, I will be waiting for you! If it is expensive for you, I can give you a discount on my reading. I know, I asked about the reading, but the woman we were spoken about, she has to apologize. I am not going to support a woman who calls me slow and retarded. I have feelings too, and she was OK. Honey, as you wish, and if you need my help, you can turn to me at anytime! and I will also be ready to give you a good discount on my readings! I was really OK, and she spoke back in the reading, "OK, so you want to speak with me now? I said not yet, but soon. and she was like, "OK dear, come to me anytime then! I was OK. I'll be responding to this reading: I was curious about what was going on with me.

77. coming future

What was happening to me and why did the readings have to continue I was just thinking about what the near future might hold for me. And what Rose saw for me in my love life was paw. Please understand that paw bm is not my love life. Rose said back to me, "Hello, Anastacia, there are changes coming into my life right now! The stars and planets affect many aspects of life! You should be aware of what you are preparing for in order to stay in tune with myself and be on the right path! I can't wait to go over the key points with me and take my life up a notch! And if I have issues with financials, I'm ready to give you a good coupon on your next read! I hope you are fine now. I told her thanks. But can she tell me what I have to be prepared for and who? I'm sorry, she said, but my free reading time is limited! Just come to me when you are ready to know more details. And also, I feel there are just enough good changes! Don't worry about that!

78. I could never be weak

I had to tell Reina I was not weak for this man paw, and I heard several times that he could leave me, but oh well, I'm thinking he could, but I'ma live my life with or without him. As Reina said to me, "My dear, you are very strong energetically. You give off a powerful charge, and he takes advantage of it because he depends on you energetically and feeds on your energy and weakens it. I basically said, "It's not my fault, but if he stops messing with other women and stops disrespecting me like I'm an invisible person to him. Reina was saying, "Honey, you misunderstood me. He can't do it without you and your energy, because he feeds on it. I told her I don't understand why he's feeding off my energy. She was going to say because you are stronger than him and he gets a charge of energy from you. All people are divided into those who give and those who receive energy, and someone is necessarily dependent on someone energetically.

79. energetic level

It's something about how paw wants to mess with me on an energetic level. I'm not sure why he thinks he has to come fuck with me on an energetic level and he's not proving anything because he doesn't have anything to prove for this situation on why he relied so heavily on my energy. and I told paw time and time again that I didn't want to be with him. and he is looking for support from me. And I don't know why he is looking for money from me because, essentially, it has come to a close dead end with us in person. I already knew this. I have knowledge. paw hurt me and I cried several times because of his messed-up, cold-hearted, toxic ways. I don't want anything like that to support a nigga like him who fucks clean over me, and I believe I don't. It's not that simple just to get up and leave paw that easily.

80. no readings

No, I do not need those readings. These readings were unnecessary for me. My life was already something I knew about for myself and paw because he was the main character in everything we did as a couple. But we will never settle down for nothing, but it will always be private between us romantically and sexually. It was the first time he did something enormously to me and left me high and dry after sex because he had someone in the car waiting on him, and I didn't appreciate it at all because he had to go and couldn't stay long. He gets on my nerves, but half the time he gets on my nerves, some of the things he does to make get on my nerves, sometimes I get tired of some of the shit he puts me through and it sickens me. It's some shit that makes me upset about what he wants to keep doing, and he keeps on repeating all the way to the max-extreme, it will never fail or change for us. I am done and fed up.

81. Why is he oblivious

Why is he oblivious to what paw wants to get away with me? He never wants to man up and be a boss with me, but I have to act like a lady and think like a man for him. Well, I am not a man. I have to project manage his ass because if I don't, his spirit wife might get in the way. If I don't project manage paw because he will go on and on and on with the same old shit and he never stops with this same shit over the years we have been sleeping with each other, he wants a threesome. And why is it a threesome? Because we're not having a threesome with your cousin Lee Lee, who claims she's not like that, but she'll be a brave nigga to have one with me and Paw, who claims to be classic like Cardi B. Cardi B is a daring lady, though. But this is the reason why paw is so extra with what he wants to do with us. I'ma keep this one hundred ego because basically I'ma be this ego for myself too, and that's how it's going to be for me because I ain't having this threesome with paw, nope!

82. spirit says

I'm not using another name for this energy paw has with me, so I'm going to go on and say, Dear, the spirit says that there is a strong energetic connection between me and him. Paw has a strong connection with me and him, so from my understanding, I'm not removed from Paw's life, which means I'm still his woman for life and will always be his woman forever. I'm not going anywhere. I am his lover and will always be paww lover, so these ugly women can get with it because I'm here to stay because I can. energetic connection. What does that mean? But at the same time, there are some misunderstandings between me and paw, which are between him and I. paw often thinks about me. Yes, paw does, but to me, it's not good enough for me to get used by paw wanting money from me. OK, so you're saying we have a strong connection? Yes, dear. We can feel each other's energy level. Dear, a lot of important changes will come in my life soon. What he's holding me to him.

83. I am wife rolled

Oh yea, I found out I was his wife, which I already knew, so what is the point of him wanting me to be his wife, and since he played me for his other spirit wife, what is it that paw has for me? Nothing, I bet, because he will never have anything for me and nothing to show for it. I ask Hector Savage if I need to know anything else about his support from me and what he needs my support for. Honey, I've tapped into your energies, and I see that this guy generally views me from a very consumerist point of view. He wants me to protect him in every way—to be caring, like a mother and wife rolled into one. He wants to see me as a reliable friend, and at the same time, he hopes that I will help him with money. I ask, is that a good thing or a bad thing? He said, "What do I think? It's up to me, but I see that I have strong feelings for him anyway, and he wants to see him next to me. and I said yes, I do, but not what he wants. Yes, the strong feelings, but not what he wants.

84. point of views

I am not a point of view because I am not paw wife or mother-to-be. I'm not going to go for this problem, hun. I've got enough problems without worrying about a man like Paw, and I don't need his problems. He has twelve children, or how many he has. Dude, I'm not a step mother to any of paw children, and I'm not going to be. Listen up, listen up! Paw wants money from me for all his children. Where in the hell did poor mother Chasity's mind go? She doesn't want me to hurt her son paw. How am I hurting this man when he refuses to do anything for me and paw isn't keeping me safe from women? But Chasity has to say she doesn't want me to hurt her son, but I'ma get to that part. But just let me say some more about paw. Why in the world would I help paw take care of his bm's children? Is Paw insane to say that he has to command and demand my help, but I will not allow paw to take power and steal my pride?

85. I am not his view wife

Hector says! He wants me, but he has very different intentions. Not like mines. Do I want to know more? I said, "Yea, I do. OK, I will soon. " Hector said, "OK, dear, I am waiting for you. I have to say, what you mean he wants me, so you're saying he wants me by sex, so by giving him money to use me to take his spirit wife shopping with my money, I don't think so, and all of this is negative to me. Hector says, "No, this is too much. It's not all that bad. I told Hector I don't think so. I don't mind getting the reading to find out. I'll be back soon. He replies, "Hi dear. We can continue today. I will be glad to see you at the reading. It's me again, but not right now. I couldn't get into the reading until I was ready, but I will soon because I want to know more about paw. Paw has gone insane thinking I'm just a view wife and stepmother rolled into one. I don't think I am this. I am not going to run behind paw at all. I can't believe that he will look up to me as nothing to him. Why would paw treat me so wrongly?

86. a mother to him

Speaking to Crystal: Hello there, welcome and thank you. I hope all is well. I see that he thinks he can treat you how he wants because he knows you are a nice person and will give him chances. I don't feel there is much of a connection between you. I feel you will end up being like a mother to him, as opposed to any partner. Yes, me! I would like to know what kind of mother I could be to him because I'm damn sure not a stepmother. I could be paw next baby mother in the furure. But if I'm just a mother to him, he'll just be a father and husband to me as well as a nice person. Paw thinks if I'm going to be a nice person to the point where he thinks I'm just going to accept him back for intimacy, paw has another thing coming because I ain't all that nice for him to come by just to use me for support. He thinks I'ma just support him, but that will be something that I am not and will not be to him. He will not get what I have.

87. close to me

According to what my reader was telling me when I asked, Paw wants to be close to me now, so he needs me to be close to him. Why? Is he up to something? If he has to be close to me by needing me for support, then that's the only way we are going to get close by paw needing support from me because that's the only thing I can see to keep the relationship going because I don't see where anything of this is coming from or going anywhere. This is just going to push me far away from him and make me never want to sleep with him ever again. If that's the case, he needs money from me. He was tapping into the energies and, OK, he said, "I see that he needs your attention. I don't see anything suspicious, but to me, I see things suspicious from my end point of view." OK, he said, "He needs your support and I was saying what kind of attention and he was saying dear, "Come to my session and I will tell you more about him and how he feels. OK! He said it again. support.

88. support

Hi, how are you? Come to my session, dear. I have something new to tell you. I was thinking to myself, "Paw doesn't need any support." So when the reader said, "Support," I was curious as to what he meant. I assumed he meant just being there when he wants some, which he can have when he comes over to me to provide him with this pussy when he needs it. But he wants money, and I don't have a choice but to give him this pussy and no money. It was my pleasure to meet him. I gave all the affectionate paw needed. Serving to give is the best way to please my dear, and I thought that was good enough to please him, but I see paw is just not pleased, even when he comes to get some. He wants me to give him money, and where does he get the idea that he can treat me this way? He is a bad person to me, and he isn't good enough to be asking for my help.

89. come to use me

Paww Mother Chasity appears to be using me in the same way that her son is attempting to play that nice role. I'm not slow, but I ran across something: "I'm fine. I have a question to ask." Yes, sure. Someone said, and I said, My mother-in-law's name is Chasity. I date her son from time to time paw, and she is on my Facebook page. His mother will view my videos sometimes, but not regularly. But what is on her mind about me? I know we had a beef out in the past over Facebook and she said something about me to her son. I want to know about Miss Chasity. Thank you for giving the dates. Let me ask my spirits. You should wait for the spirits' answer. OK, sorry, spirits' question: do you want to know Miss Chasity's attitude towards you? Is that all? I should tell Spirits the reason for asking. Yea, OK, dear, just a second, OK,

90. passing on facebook

I can see that this woman is interested in your life. She is looking for you on social media to get more information about you. I see her passing by your house all the time. but maybe. She is dreaming of passing by your home as often as it's possible. Chasity passed by my home page on social media, so it couldn't be where I live, where she wants to come over to see me to get close, so the information she wants to know about me would be on Facebook. To finish up the reading, at any rate, I see the image of a woman coming by your home. She is not inclined to do something bad for you. She is trying to get more information about you and outlines common topics for conversation to get closer to you. But does she know I'm her daughter-in-law? She knows, but she does not know you indeed as a person. It is easier for her to pass by your home and watch your manner of speaking and behavior than to ask you an exact question.

91. on social media

Chasity, paw mother. She is dreaming because I don't have time for her son, so she could be dreaming as she passes by my Facebook home page. This is where my home page is on Facebook and nothing else. I hope Chasity got something interesting for me because her son isn't, but I have nothing for her or her son paw, so whatever it is, I ain't giving. But the reading was not given to me by any means. She wants to know what kind of person I am. But she is doing it in her own manner, which may be a little strange for us. Yes, she can do it in her own manner because her son paw isn't giving her a chance and opportunity to get to know me as the good person that I am, and she will never know me if she doesn't do it in her own manner. So, chasity is right. She would have to keep looking and trying to find out because it's not going to get her anywhere.

92. It's my decision

Chasity is trying to get close to me on social media, but oh well, if that's what she's trying to do, she is more than welcome to look at almost everything I do for a living on my home page on social media. So she's trying to get close to me. Well, do you mean to get me to come by her house? said, It's my decision. I wanted to know what was on her mind. I think I know it myself. I don't need no any spirits for that. At any rate, this woman is not going to do me any harm. OK, thanks. The spirit says that she is really watching all my pictures and videos. She is scared that I will hurt him. Is she trying to reach me? Yes, she is going to talk with me. I said, "This is very unnecessary. She thinks I'm going to hurt her son paw, but I didn't do anything to hurt him. Most likely, Paw does the most out of all of what he does all the time, and I never get an apology for his karmic ways.

93. reliable friend

Why do paw see me as a reliable friend when there is no clarity in this toxic reliable friend thing? And ask me this: why is it that it has to be so complicated with him that he has to make things so suspicious If he is up against something, why is he looking for money from me when it is so important to paw? And why is that because I have so much to say about him? Because this is what it leads up to this. I don't understand why I have to be a reliable friend when he is ready to come see me. Why does he wants money? I feel he should be a reliable friend to me. I want to keep it low. He is very toxic and cannot do this. I shouldn't trust him. What if it's too late and he does this to me again? It's not about money topics. I don't want to be with him like that, giving him money. I hope he stops! I've been hurt by him, and he doesn't understand that.

94. not reliable

Paw wants me to be a reliable friend to him, but he can't be a reliable friend to me. And I don't know really why he wants money from me when he's not being a reliable friend to me. Paw is not really being fair with us and he always thinks I have a boyfriend, but really when he comes over, Paw is the only man I mess with at all times when he wants a reliable friend, but he needs to understand it's not me that I need to be a reliable friend to him, and I hope Paww stops with all the lies that I need to be his reliable friend when he needs someone like me to care for and provide for him because it seems to me that paw wants me to be his reliable friend. That's something like a get over using me problem when he needs a hand to lean on, a hand full of money to give to paw. And no, he is not getting it.

95. keep it low

In other words, paw may want to keep it low with us. Hey, as I previously stated, there are no advantages to having sex with us, no money, no advantages! OK, baby, keep it low! paw would have to keep it low. There is no need to force things. It will come naturally. But for now, he will remain with me until he matures into a better man. I sent him a text to tell him to keep it low with us because if he can't protect me from his bms, there is no friendship between us. He really needs to keep it low because that was something he was not trying to do with me. Keep it low for us and I'm not going to be a fool or a slow dummy person. He wants me to come run behind him so he can do whatever he wants. The Lord knows what he might end up doing in front of me. It's a time to keep things low with us, and forever until then, there would be no us.

96. not reliable enough

Now I'm going to ask my cards about your friend, and no, paw is not my friend. I can see that I'm very discouraged by my friendship. My friend is not reliable enough, and I feel he is taking advantage of me. I will not let him do that, even if he tries to. This will not happen if paw tries to take advantage of me. I see he's up to something against me. It seems to be about money. can tell it's important. It doesn't seem to be very important to me that paw needs any money if I don't see him more often as a friend should. Paw is not getting this reward. This is something that should not be given to him easily because there is no such thing that should be handed to him. Money should be handed with care, not with disrespect to give him the money while paw going out with other women behind my back. What would I like to know? I'm waiting, dear. I'll get the reading later. I can see that it might get too late and he will do this to me again.

97. readings

To me, these readings were experiences to know how these readers felt about me and paw and why things were not valuable between us and there was no reliable friendship at the end to see each other and tune in to everything. OK, thank you. Well, thank me. Yes, thank me! Dear, I feel that everything is quite good between us. No it wasn't. It was not good between us. He is trying to be closer to me, but being closer isn't going to make anything better between us because I think I should just leave because paw got too much baggage. He needs me. We need to be together. He needs to be careful with me because I am very serious. It really doesn't make any sense to want us to be close when paw wants to do the opposite but doesn't want to make anything happen for us. This reading was to build my intuitive to know what others feel about me and to know our life experiences more.

98. lonely aura

I see that I have a lonely aura, but this person definitely has an interest in me. At the same time, he is careful. No, I'm not lonely. I'm just by myself. I'm not hurt about it. What is he careful about? because I have a strong character, and he sees it. This scares him because he is not as strong as he wants to appear. One thing about me is that I could never be lonely because I'd rather be alone instead of attending some drama family that causes so much mess, and I prefer being a strong woman for myself instead of being in a relationship that doesn't fit me very well. Being a reliable friend first does not come naturally. I don't see how someone like paw would think so easily that being a reliable friend is true. Reliable friends do not come with slut bags and I'm not one of them. I'm not falling for paw mistakes because he does it very well and he ain't going to do it very well with me.

99. repeating mistakes

I think that paw will never change for the better, that he wants to keep repeating mistakes, that he wants to be with someone else and not me, so I can do better by myself, to make it by myself single and happy, and I can't imagine that things will work out as paw planned because I am normally not accepting of the things he wants, because it's not something that properly will not happen. Why would he want me to do things that are not normal for me to do? That's something that's not going to happen to him. I will never do it. He cannot have those wishes from me. Why would I do those things about giving him money when I had then left him? My money is very valuable and it's not to be shared by others who cannot have it. It's called "breaking the code," and paw will not receive it. Money doesn't come with a silver platter, something that just goes away.

100. toxic intimacy

Paw would like to see me as an over-the-top woman wife. It's out of my lead and he will never see things how he would want them to be because it's not his will to receive them. Why does he come into my life with so much toxic intimacy and the part of his plan is that he does things so surprisingly toxic and unexpected? I know he has something ready, and I know he's going to have something big. I don't know what it is, but it's coming soon. I know it's going to happen. Only time will tell when it's going to happen because this man is something else. Why is he doing these strange things? He is going to build a wall between us. I know this is a huge blockage. He's not going to do anything but strengthen me. But if this is what he wants to build a wall between us, then that is on him and now guess what? I can live my life with a free will to do what the fuck I want.

9 789356 670587